MANCHESTER
OLD AND NEW

FRANK MULLINEUX

EP Publishing Limited

01142978
44016758

This edition first published 1975
by EP Publishing Limited
East Ardsley, Wakefield, West Yorkshire
England

ISBN: 0 7158 1080 4

Please address all enquiries to EP Publishing Limited
(address as above)

Printed in Great Britain by Fretwell & Brian Limited
Silsden, Keighley, West Yorkshire

PUBLISHER'S NOTE:-
The captions on pages 38 and 40
should be transposed.

Author's Introduction

Manchester has frequently, and rightly, been referred to as a Victorian City, but during that period a few buildings of the older Manchester survived to be photographed by the small group of early photographers who recognised the importance of recording the Manchester of 'Then'.

The City of Manchester Central Library has built up a splendid collection of photographs and I am grateful to Mr David Taylor, the Local History Librarian and his staff for the courtesy and help I received whilst searching for photographs. With the exception of two pictures all the old illustrations are from the Library Collection.

I am especially grateful to my friend Mr Arnold S. Day for taking all the new photographs, mostly under difficult and sometimes very cold conditions and for copying two photographs by S.L. Coulthurst, pages 27 and 71.

Following reconstruction after bomb damage and a massive re-development in many cases, of the City, the townscapes and skyline have given it an almost new identity. There remain however, many fine examples of Victorian architecture which can well be seen by riding on the upper deck of a 'bus.

All the illustrations have been, more or less, confined to the central area.

Frank Mullineux,
Worsley, 1975

Contents

MANCHESTER
OLD AND NEW

Market Place from the entrance to St. Ann's Square - 1878 *(photo A. Brothers)*
The nucleus of ancient Manchester was in this area. Whilst from the 18th century Manchester grew rapidly the Market Place remained. Despite Victorian buildings replacing older properties a few survived. The area was devastated during an air raid in December 1940 and its long existence as a market ended.

1

Market Place from the entrance to St. Ann's Square - 1974
A few modern buildings have been erected but the total development of the old Market Place area as a complex
of shops, offices, stores and car park is progressing.

Market Place - 1897

(photo S. L. Coulthurst)

In the background is the new Royal Exchange with its tower and dome. On the left is a Skittle Alley and Shooting Range, the range being in the cellars. On the right a little of an old timber framed building, The Wellington Inn, is shown. This was a private house until 1830. In the first half of the 18th century it was the home of John Byrom who very probably wrote his famous hymn 'Christians Awake' there.

Market Place - 1974
The tower of the Royal Exchange shows, for the present, above the building work noted on page 2. The Wellington Inn survived the bombing and because of its architectural and historic importance was not allowed to be demolished. It has been raised and its position moved slightly. The inn, encased for protection, can be seen behind the crane-tower.

St. Mary's Gate - 1896
Leading from Deansgate to Market Street, St. Mary's Gate had been lined by old properties which were replaced by the huge Victoria Buildings on the left between 1870 and 1880.

5

St. Mary's Gate - 1974
The first building on the left, Marks and Spencer's modern store, covers an area of old alleys and part of the old Market Place.

St. Ann's Square - c. 1866.
The square, previously Acresfield, was, as an open field, the scene of an annual fair. In the 18th century it became an elegant residential square and later, a fashionable shopping area. St. Ann's Church, the gift of Lady Ann Bland, was built in 1712 for those who preferred a plainer service than those at the Cathedral. In 1745 Prince Charles Edward Stewart's soldiers were reviewed in the square. On the extreme left is 'John Fletcher and Others, Atherton Coal Office' and next but one, 'E.L. Fleming, Photographer'.

St. Ann's Square - 1974
Still a much favoured shop and office area. Shortly it is intended to exclude vehicles. The church originally was
surmounted by a cupola.

8

St. Ann's Square - 1895

The entrance to the square from St. Mary's Gate was originally along a narrow alley. This was replaced by Exchange Street which runs alongside the Royal Exchange, Manchester's third exchange building. In the centre of the square is the statue of Richard Cobden to commemorate his Free Trade reforms, so advantageous to Manchester's trade.

St. Ann's Square - 1974
New office blocks and shops and modernised shop fronts are today a feature. On the right the Royal Exchange building dominates the entrance but with the contraction of the Lancashire cotton trade it is no longer the hub of the textile industry. In the main hall it is proposed to establish a theatre.

Market Street - 1914
Known until the early 19th century as Market Stede (Place) Lane it was a street of shops and houses which had expanded from the Market Place area. Originally a very narrow street it was widened and the properties rebuilt at a cost of some £250,000 between 1822 and 1834. The photograph was taken from the corner of Cross Street and shows a daily scene of activity.

Market Street - 1974
On the corner of Cross Street development of the area which included the 'Manchester Guardian' building is in progress. In the distance is the 1930s building of the great merchant firm of Rylands, now occupied by Debenham's.

Market Street - c. 1890
A street of shops and offices with the Royal Exchange Tower visible at the lower end. It was one of the busiest streets in the period of prosperity when 'What Manchester thinks today London thinks tomorrow.' The photograph is taken from the corner of High Street.

Market Street - 1974
Some of the old buildings remain but with the shop fronts modernised, some would say 'tarted up'.

Deansgate - c.1890

This road, the way into the town from the SW, is one of the oldest, the further end being on the line of a Roman road. Deansgate was widened in 1869. The photograph shows, in the foreground, the corner of John Dalton Street and the handsome Victorian buildings erected after the widening. Note the 'penny-farthing' bicycle.

15

Deansgate - 1974
Kendal Milne's (Harrod's Ltd) designed by J. W. Beaumont and Son was a notable addition to Deansgate in 1939.
It stands as a good example of department store design opposite to the firm's old building.

16

Deansgate - c.1878
The section of Deansgate leading to Victoria Street and the Cathedral. On the left is the shop of Walmsley and Son, Hatters above which is the National Boiler Insurance office. On the right is the shop of a brush manufacturer.

Deansgate - 1974
Office development on the left continues down to the river bank. It replaces amongst other buildings the Grosvenor Hotel and the fire-destroyed Deansgate Hotel. On the right the area of the Victoria Hotel and Buildings destroyed by bombing in 1940 is being built up anew.

Exchange Station - c.1905

The statue of Oliver Cromwell was placed, in 1875, on this spot near to where, it is said, the first fatality in the Civil War occurred. To ease the traffic flow the statue was removed a few years ago, to the grounds of Wythenshawe Hall. The bridge spanning the River Irwell leads to Exchange Station built by the London and North Western Railway Co. in 1884. From this station the world's longest railway platform connected it with Victoria Station.

Exchange Station - 1974
The forecourt and offices were badly damaged during an air raid in World War II. The station is now closed, not because of the damage, but rationalisation has directed services to the Victoria Station which was the station of the old Lancashire and Yorkshire Railway Co.

The River Irwell and Victoria Bridge - c.1938
Victoria Bridge, opened in 1839 and named after the recently crowned Queen Victoria, replaced the inadequate old Salford Bridge which had stood for centuries as Manchester's only bridge over the river. On the left is the back of the Grosvenor Hotel and in the visible gap was the back of the Deansgate Hotel. In the 1930s it was gutted by fire and lives were lost by people trying to escape by leaping into the river. On the right is the extensive building of James Woolley, pharmaceutical manufacturers and suppliers.

The River Irwell and Victoria Bridge - 1974
New office development is going on along both banks of the river. The nearest building on the right is the high-rise Highland House with its unusual window decoration. On the near side of the bridge is an unsightly 'bus shelter.

The River Irwell and Blackfriars Bridge - 1821
Through the 18th and 19th centuries the river was used for carrying goods to and from the works in Manchester and Salford and along its route, even to Liverpool. Pleasure boats plied from near this point to the Pomona Gardens at Old Trafford. The wooden bridge was built by a company of actors to give easier access to their playhouse on the Salford side (the right). The church of St. Mary was consecrated in 1756. Eventually it was demolished.

The River Irwell and Blackfriars Bridge - 1974
The new bridge was subject to the payment of tolls until the cost had been recovered. Now the banks are lined with office blocks. The river is said to be showing a slight improvement in the intensity of its pollution. In the last century its filthiness led to a rhyme 'The Irwell, the Irk and ink, All three are liquids but none is fit to drink'.

Long Millgate - 1866. *(photo G. Grundy)*
Some of Manchester's older buildings surviving along one of the town's oldest streets. In the background is the east end of the Cathedral.

Long Millgate - 1974
On the right is the building, c. 1870, which housed the famous Manchester Grammar School which moved in the 1930s to a new school. Now it is used as a College of Education. The east end of the Cathedral, now restored by splendid craftsmanship, was severly damaged by bombing in World War II.

Withy Grove - 1889

(photo S. L. Coulthurst)

Samuel Coulthurst, an amateur photographer, was taking 'candid camera' photographs at this early date in the streets. Whilst producing 'character studies' his photographs sometimes give glimpses of the streets themselves as in the case of Withy Grove leading to Shudehill.

Withy Grove - 1974
On the left is the newspaper office, Thompson House, formerly the headquarters of the old 'Daily Dispatch'. The area of rebuilding is bounded in the distance by High Street and on the right by Cannon Street.

Oxford Road at All Saints - 1892   *(photo S. J. Bradburn)*
One of the principal roads into the city from the south. On the left was All Saints Church standing in a residential square originally.

29

Oxford Road at All Saints - 1974
The church of All Saints was damaged by bombing. The site was cleared and is now a tree-lined open space.
The bridge over the road carries the Mancunian Way, a motorway through the heart of the city. In the centre of the
picture is the chief office of the Refuge Assurance Co., with its clock tower.

Chapel Street, Salford - 1889 *(photo S. L. Coulthurst)*
Although in Salford, this point is almost on the boundary with Manchester and has for centuries been the road into Manchester from the west. On the left is Sacred Trinity Church. For a long period a traditional market was held on the pavement surrounding the triangular site of the church, hence the soubriquet 'The Flat Iron Market'.

Chapel Street, Salford - 1974
From the 17th century there has been a Sacred Trinity Church but there was a building in 1751 followed by Victorian alterations. In the distance are the C.I.S. offices, Manchester's first really tall building, erected in 1962. Rising above the buildings in the centre is Highland House, 1966, which stands on the riverside at Victoria Bridge.

London Road Station - 1957
Built in 1842 by the London and North Western Railway Co., as their terminus from the south it was jointly opera-
ted along with the Manchester, Sheffield and Lincoln Railway Company.

33

Piccadilly Station - 1974
London Road Station was re-named and rebuilt by British Railways. New offices and a new concourse had been completed by 1966 when the new electrified line was opened to London. Two years later the curving office and shops building along the station approach was completed.

Newton Street - c.1885
Leading off Piccadilly the street ran into an area of warehouses and industrial buildings.

Newton Street - 1974
At the turn of the century Manchester's expansion led to the need for more office and shop accommodation.

Piccadilly - c.1885

The old name for the road was Lever's Row but the name Piccadilly was in use in the early 19th century. On the left stands the Infirmary, the first infirmary building on this site was opened in 1755. It underwent several additions and many alterations. The wide pavement was laid out over a large pond. Piccadilly links Market Street and London Road and has for over 200 years been a place where Manchester people have sat and relaxed.

Piccadilly - 1974
Behind the gardens a luxury hotel and office blocks have replaced the warehouses which were devastated in the Manchester 'blitz' of 1940. The Hansom cabs have been replaced by a taxi stand and 'bus shelters line two sides of the area.

Piccadilly - 1910 *(photo J. Shaw)*
The final remains of the old infirmary can be seen behind the Hansom cabs. Behind the site, large warehouses of the 19th century.

Piccadilly - 1974
On the site of the old infirmary temporary library buildings were erected and when these were removed the Piccadilly Gardens were created. The building to the right of the statue was the Piccadilly Cinema, 1922. In the 1920s it was Manchester's largest cinema. The tall building on the right is the Manchester headquarters of the B.B.C.

St. Peter's Square - c.1913
The site of St. Peter's Church is marked by the cross. Business premises line the sqaure with the Midland Hotel standing on Peter Street.

41

St. Peter's Square - 1974
The square was completely remodelled and the great Central Library, designed by Vincent Harris, was opened in 1934.

Lower Mosley Street - c.1895

(photo S. L. Coulthurst)

On the extreme right is the Casino Music Hall and next to it stands the Day and Sunday Schools started in 1789 by members of the Cross Street Chapel. In the background is part of the 210 ft. span of Central Station opened in 1880 used by the Great Northern Railway, the Cheshire Lines Committee and the Midland Railway.

Lower Mosley Street - 1974
The Midland Hotel, a ten-storey building of granite, terra-cotta and brick, was designed by Charles Trubshaw for the Midland Railway in 1898. The railway station is now closed and many efforts have been made to prevent its demolition. Beneath the station the Manchester and Salford Junction Canal ran underground.

Albert Square - c.1895   *(photo S. L. Coulthurst)*
In the middle of the 19th century this was an area of industrial buildings and houses. In the twenty years before 1880 it had completely changed. Right of the statue of John Bright there is a fountain behind which is an inn built on the site of the house where the author Thomas de Quincey lived.

45

Albert Square - 1974
New buildings erected early this century alter the view at the corner of John Dalton Street and Cross Street. The trees were presented to the City a few years ago by the Manchester Evening News.

Mount Street - c.1890
Leading to Albert Square this short wide street gives a good view, with the Albert Memorial designed by the Manchester architect Thomas Worthington in 1867, as the central feature. The great Town Hall completed in 1877 to the design of Alfred Waterhouse is surmounted by the fine tower. On the left the iron rails stand in front of the Meeting House of the Society of Friends.

Mount Street - 1974
The building on the right is part of the Town Hall extensions completed in 1938 in which the architect Vincent Harris provided a sympathetic link between the old Town Hall and the new library.

Campfield Market - 1914

In the 19th century the Market Place was inadequate and other large markets for specialised purposes, such as vegetables and meat, had been established. At Campfield (Liverpool Road on the left and Byrom Street on the right) hay and straw amongst other things were sold. Behind is the tower of St. John's Church.

49

The City Exhibition Hall - 1974
Built partly of iron and glass the Hall houses many types of commercial exhibitions. It is on the site of
Campfield Market. Campfield, an old name, derives from its nearness to the Roman fort.

St. John Street - c.1910
At right angles to Deansgate the street was a fashionable residential area. At the end of the street was
St John's Church.

St. John Street - 1974
The street is now the 'Harley Street' of Manchester. Each of the gracious Georgian houses has consulting rooms of doctors and surgeons. St. John's Church has been demolished and the site preserved as a green area.

Bridge Street West - 1952
Just on the Manchester side of the River Irwell, the boundary with Salford, this group of shops was familiar to thousands of commuters using Salford Station.

Bridge Street West - 1974
The removal of the shops has opened up the view of Crown Square showing the side of the new Crown Courts built in 1962.

Albert Bridge and River Irwell - c.1920
On the left bank is the landing stage and boat-house of the Nemesis Rowing Club. In the 19th century a number of rowing clubs used the river. On the left are the goods offices and marshalling yards of the Lancashire and Yorkshire Railway Co., which were built on the site of the New Bailey prison. Bridge Street from Salford into Manchester crosses Albert Bridge.

Albert Bridge and River Irwell - 1974
On the left is Aldine House, 1967, known as West Riverside. Other office block building is almost completed opposite to Aldine House.

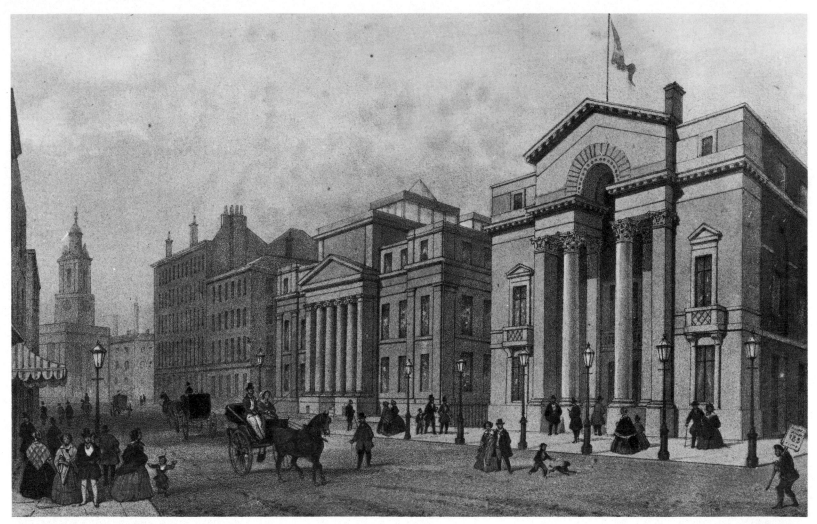

Peter Street - 1855

On the right is the third Theatre Royal in Manchester - the others were not on this site. It was opened in 1845 and later Sir Henry Irving appeared in Shakespearean plays in this theatre. Immediately left of the theatre is the Museum of the Manchester Natural History Society opened in 1851. In the distance is St. Peter's Church, 1794, standing in St. Peter's Square which at that time was on the fringe of the town.

Peter Street - 1974
The Theatre Royal used as a cinema stands on the right. The Museum has been replaced by the Y.M.C.A. building erected in 1909. On the site of St. Peter's Church is the first World War Memorial designed by Lutyens in 1924.

Peter Street - 1959

The Gaiety Theatre, opened in 1884, was the home of one of the first Repertory Companies, run by Miss Horniman from 1908 to 1921. In the company were actors such as Basil Dean, Sybil Thorndike and her husband Lewis Casson who eventually achieved fame. This progressive company helped the playwrights, Harold Brighouse, Alan Monkhouse and Stanley Houghton who became known as the 'Manchester School'. The theatre had an important place in the annals of the theatre in Britain but eventually it became a cinema and was demolished in 1959.

Peter Street - 1974
Offices and shops on the site of the Gaiety Theatre.

Oxford Street - c.1938
The Prince's Theatre, delightfully decorated inside in cream and gold with blue velvet upholstered seats and lace head rests, was built about 1860 and many famous actors appeared there. It became recognised as the place for musical comedies. It suffered in the bombing of Manchester and was demolished.

Oxford Street - 1974
Peter House now occupies the site of the Prince's Theatre. It is the headquarters of the Clerical, Medical and General Life Assurance Company.

Oxford Street - 1935
The Hippodrome, the home of Variety shows and 'spectaculars', moved out to Ardwick and the site was used on which to build a cinema.

63

Oxford Street - 1974
Built in the late 1930s on the site of the Hippodrome the Gaumont was at that time Manchester's most up-to-date cinema with its Long Bar and Mezzanine. It is now standing empty.

Oxford Street - 1934
Leading to St. Peter's Square, Oxford Street, with Peter Street, had long been 'Theatre Street' in Manchester.

Oxford Street - 1974
New office blocks, shops and the Odeon Cinema and a recent crop of cafes and restaurants almost enclose
St. Peter's Square but do not blot out the Central Library.

Sackville Street - 1910
On arches, the Cheshire Lines Committee Railway runs in front of the Manchester College of Technology.
This great institution has played a notable part in the life of Manchester industry.

Sackville Street - 1974
The railway arches still run in front of the old building of the Manchester College of Technology but in the last thirty years it has become one building in the extensive complex of the University of Manchester Institute of Technology. Some of the new departments stand on the right whilst on the left are a car park and the Swinging Sporran, doubtless amenities for the students.

Stevenson Square - 1891
The square was intended as an elegant residential area but industry and commerce altered its use. It became
an area of warehouses, factories and packing buildings. As an open space it was, before and after 1900, a notable
place for all manner of meetings, especially those of a political sort.

Stevenson Square - 1974
Lying between Piccadilly and Oldham Street the square is still commercially used and is the terminus for 'buses to Oldham and places N.E. of Manchester.

Shudehill - 1889

(photo S. L. Coulthurst)

At the junction of Shudehill and Swan Street, the one with its poultry market and the other with its vegetable market, the photographer has captured the period: the street piano, the lorry, the stalls and the sign 'Lamp Maker'.

Shudehill - 1974
The markets are gone and the internal combustion engine has taken over.

Minshull Street - 1920
One of the works, that of the Manchester Patent Ice Company, still lingering near the City centre. The site is at the junction with Whitworth Street.

Minshull Street - 1974
The frontage of this building is on Aytoun Street near the junction with Whitworth Street and houses some departments of the Manchester Polytechnic.